Te
Are
Temporary

Charles L. Allen

A BARBOUR BOOK

Published by **Barbour and Company, Inc.**
   P.O. Box 719
   Uhrichsville, Ohio 44683

Typeset by Typetronix, Fort Myers, FL

ISBN   1-55748-347-7

Printed in the United States of America

1   2   3   4   5 / 98   97   96   95   94   93

Acknowledgments

QUOTATION FROM *CHANGING TIMES* REPRINTED BY PERMISSION FROM THE DECEMBER 1968 ISSUE OF *CHANGING TIMES MAGAZINE* COPYRIGHT © 1968 THE KIPLINGER WASHINGTON EDITORS, INC.

SELECTIONS FROM *GRIT* REPRINTED WITH PERMISSION FROM *GRIT*, COPYRIGHT 1969, GRIT PUBLISHING GROUP, TOPEKA, KANSAS.

QUOTATION FROM EDWARD K. BOK REPRINTED WITH PERMISSION OF CHARLES SCRIBNER'S SONS, AN IMPRINT OF MACMILLIAN PUBLISHING COMPANY FROM *TWICE THIRTY* BY EDWARD K. BOK. COPYRIGHT 1925 CHARLES SCRIBNER'S SONS; COPYRIGHT RENEWED 1953 MARY LOUIS CURTIS ZIMBALIST.

QUOTATION FROM HERBERT V. PROCHNOW AND HERBERT V. PROCHNOW, JR. USED BY PERMISSION OF HERBERT V. PROCHOW.

QUOTATION FROM J. C. MACAULAY TAKEN FROM *MOODY MAGAZINE'S* JUNE 1969 ARTICLE "THE WARRING FAITH" BY J. C. MACAULAY. COPYRIGHT 1969 MOODY BIBLE INSTITUTE OF CHICAGO. MOODY PRESS. USED BY PERMISSION.

QUOTATION FROM GREGORY R. ANRIG REPRINTED WITH PERMISSION, FROM *THE AMERICAN SCHOOL BOARD JOURNAL*, OCTOBER 1969. COPYRIGHT 1969, THE NATIONAL SCHOOL BOARDS ASSOCIATION. ALL RIGHT RESERVED.

QUOTATION FROM *THE RAILWAY CLERK* REPRINTED WITH PERMISSION FROM THE TRANSPORTATION COMMUNICATIONS UNION.

QUOTATION FROM KENNETH ROBERTS TAKEN FROM *OLIVER WISWELL* BY KENNETH ROBERTS ANNA ROBERTS. COPYRIGHT 1940 BY KENNETH ROBERTS AND ANNA M. ROBERTS. USED BY PERMISSION OF DOUBLEDAY, A DIVISION OF BANTAM DOUBLEDAY DELL PUBLISHING GROUP, INC.

QUOTATION FROM DAISY BROWN USED BY PERMISSION OF DAISY BROWN.

QUOTATIONS FROM WALTER MACPEEK TAKEN FROM *SCOUT LEADER'S IN ACTION* BY WALTER G. MACPEEK. COPYRIGHT © 1969 BY ABINGDON PRESS. EXCERPTS BY PERMISSION.

QUOTATION FROM RICHARD ARMOUR USED COURTESY OF *NEA TODAY* PUBLISHED BY THE NATIONAL EDUCATION ASSOCIATION.

QUOTATION FROM LEEWIN B. WILLIAMS TAKEN FROM *THE ENCYCLOPEDIA OF WIT, WISDOM AND HUMOR*, BY LEEWIN WILLIAMS. COPYRIGHT RENEWAL © 1976 BY CHESTER WILLIAMS. USED BY PERMISSION OF THE PUBLISHER, ABINGDON PRESS.

QUOTATION FROM WALTER B. KNIGHT TAKEN FROM *KNIGHT'S TREASURY OF ILLUSTRATIONS* BY WALTER B. KNIGHT COPYRIGHT 1963. USED BY PERMISSION FROM WM. B. EERDMANS PUBLISHING CO.

QUOTATION FROM B. C. FORBES REPRINTED BY PERMISSION OF *FORBES* MAGAZINE, JUNE 15, 1968. © FORBES INC., 1968.

QUOTATION FROM MICKEY MANTLE REPRINTED COURTESY OF *SPORTS ILLUSTRATED* FROM THE DECEMBER 7, 1970, ISSUE. COPYRIGHT © 1970 TIME, INC. *SCORECARD*. EDITED BY ROBERT CREAMER. ALL RIGHTS RESERVED.

QUOTATION FROM J. LESTER HARNISH TAKEN FROM *THE MINISTER'S MANUAL*. EXCERPTS FROM *THE MINISTER'S MANUAL* BY CHARLES L. WALLIS. COPYRIGHT © 1970 BY CHARLES L. WALLIS. REPRINTED BY PERMISSION OF HARPERCOLLINS PUBLISHERS.

QUOTATION FROM KENNETH CHAFIN TAKEN FROM *THE MINISTER'S MANUAL*. EXCERPTS FROM *THE MINISTER'S MANUAL* BY CHARLES L. WALLIS. COPYRIGHT © 1970 BY CHARLES L. WALLIS. REPRINTED BY PERMISSION OF HARPERCOLLINS PUBLISHERS.

DILIGENT EFFORT HAS BEEN MADE TO LOCATE AND SECURE PERMISSIONS FOR ALL COPYRIGHTED MATERIAL INCLUDED IN THIS BOOK. IF SUCH ACKNOWLEDGMENTS HAVE BEEN INADVERTENTLY OMITTED, OR WERE NOT RECEIVED BY THE TIME OF PUBLICATION, THE PUBLISHER WOULD APPRECIATE RECEIVING FULL INFORMATION SO THAT PROPER CREDIT MAY BE GIVEN IN FUTURE EDITIONS.

Introduction

Teenagers are notorious for their ingenuous, unpredictable, irrational, and yes, sometimes unwelcome behavior . . . a fact not lost on many of their most intimate acquaintances.

Best-selling author Charles L. Allen (*Grandparents Are Great*) has compiled a delightful collection of quips, quotes, and anecdotes dealing with the ups and downs of the teenage years. If you're a teenager, the parent of a teenager, or know and love a teenager, *this book is for you.*

Don't let anyone look down on you because you are young.

1 TIMOTHY 4:12

Youth comes but once, fortunately. You couldn't stand all that abuse for a whole lifetime.

CHANGING TIMES

Teenage is the awkward age in life. They are too old for an allowance and too young for a credit card.

You are only young once, but you can stay immature almost indefinitely.

GRIT

Teenagers are young people who get too much of everything, including criticism.

SOL KENDON

TEN THINGS I WISH I HAD KNOWN
BEFORE I WAS TWENTY-ONE

1. What I was going to do for a living—what my life work would be.
2. That my health after thirty depended in large on what I ate before I was twenty-one.
3. How to take care of money.
4. The commercial asset of being neatly and sensibly dressed.
5. That habits are mighty hard to change after you're twenty-one.

6. That worthwhile things require time, patience, and work.
7. That the world would give me just about what I deserved.
8. That a thorough education not only pays better wages than hard labor, but it brings the best of everything else.
9. That my parents weren't old fogies after all.
10. That my religious faith is important.

SOURCE UNKNOWN

TEENAGERS ARE TEMPORARY

"My teenage daughter is at that awkward age," one mother said.
"She knows how to make phone calls, but not how to end them."

ANONYMOUS

Age does not always bring wisdom. Most old people think that
because they are old, they have wisdom. Youth keeps the world
alive with its dreams, hopes, ambitions.

CLARENCE DARROW

Maturity brings the wisdom that suggests that we do not have all the answers ourselves; that, maybe there are some adults, even our parents or teachers, to whose experience it might be helpful to listen and consider.

It was said of one of the most intelligent men who ever lived in New England that, when he was asked how he knew so much about everything, he replied, "By constantly realizing my own ignorance and never being afraid or ashamed to accept advice.

Maturity begins to grow when you can accept duly constituted authority without defiance.

JOHN H. MACNAUGHTEN

Demosthenes was the greatest orator of Greece at twenty-five, and at the same age Cicero was Rome's greatest speaker.

William Gladstone was a member of the British House of Commons at twenty-four. Benjamin Franklin wrote for papers at fourteen,

At eight Beethoven created astonishment by his musical ability; at thirteen Mozart was unequaled.

Pascal discovered geometry for himself at twelve. At sixteen he wrote a treatise on conic sections, and at twenty-five he published a book on atmospheric pressure.

Aggasiz began the study of science at eleven years of age, and was recognized as one of the most profound scholars of his age while yet in his twenties.

Gibbon, the great English historian, began his studies at seventeen, and at twenty-four was publishing his historical work.

Ruskin was an accomplished art critic, and had written "Modern Painters" at twenty-four.

John Wesley was a polished and forceful writer, and a skilled logician, and at twenty-four he was a professor of Greek.

Moody was preaching at eighteen, and during his twenties became one of our greatest evangelists.

William Cullen Bryant wrote "Thanatopsis" at seventeen. Tennyson's first volumes of poems appeared at twenty. Whittier was editor of *New England Review* at twenty-three; Poe's first volume was written at twenty; and Byron's appeared at seventeen. Burns was a poetic genius at twelve, and a brilliant writer at sixteen.

SOURCE UNKNOWN

In youth the days are short and the years are long; In old age the years are short and the days are long.

PANIN

TEENAGERS ARE TEMPORARY

"I am just a young man"
In other words, what thousands of men today would like to be!
A potentiality with his face to the east!
A lifetime stretching ahead!
The Book of Life with clean pages to be written on as he may elect!
"Just a young man" in a time like this: in a land like this: in a world
    like this!
In a land of opportunity where every chance beckons and every
    road invites!
A road straight and clear, and the high peaks of achievement beyond
    —with oh! so few on them! To carve out of life what one wills!
How many men there are who would gladly give all they possess to
have that chance once more!

EDWARD K. BOK

The Old say: "I remember when . . ." The young say: "What's new?"

When we get out of sympathy with the young, then I think our work in this world is over.

GEORGE MACDONALD

Forty is the old age of youth— Fifty is the youth of old age.

VICTOR HUGO

II

The average teenagers still have all the faults their parents outgrew.

TEENAGERS ARE TEMPORARY

The main problem with teenagers is that they're just like their parents were at their age.

A boy on an overnight campout with his father was trying to lift a big rock which was on the camp site. He huffed and puffed and heaved away, but the rock wouldn't budge.

The father looked over and asked, "Son are you using all your strength?"

"Of course I am!" replied the boy.

"No, you aren't." said the father. "You haven't asked my help."

CLINTON W. RAYMOND

Teenage is when your offspring quit asking where they came from and refuse to tell you where they're going.

A father told his teenage daughter he wanted her home by 11 PM.

"But Father," she complained, "I'm no longer a child."

"I know," answered the father, "That's why I want you home by 11."

SOURCE UNKNOWN

Discussing problems concerning teenagers, one woman asked her neighbor, "Is your son hard to get out of bed in the morning?"

"No," replied the other. "I just open his door and throw the cat on his bed!"

The neighbor was puzzled. "How," she asked, "does this awaken him?"

Replied the other, "He sleeps with the dog."

GRIT

TEENAGERS ARE TEMPORARY

This is not a day when the young listen to advice from the old with much grace. In spite of that, I cannot refrain from giving this wise word from Anne Bradstreet who lived in the 17th century:

"Youth is a time of getting,—middle age of improving,—and old age of spending;"

"A negligent youth is usually attended to by an ignorant middle age, and both by an empty old age."

The thing that troubles me the most about foolish behavior on the part of the young is this, when these years are spent, they can never be recovered. Middle age and old age become ignorant and empty.

BISHOP GERALD KENNEDY

TEENAGERS ARE TEMPORARY

"Tell me how to get on in life," said the kettle.
"Take panes," said the window.
"Never be led," said the pencil.
"Do a driving business," said the hammer.
"Aspire to great things," said the nutmeg grater.
"Make light of everything," said the fire.
"Make much of small things," said the microscope.
"Never do anything offhand," said the glove.
"Reflect," said the mirror.
"Do the work you are suited for," said the chimney.
"Be sharp," said the knife.
"Find a good thing and stick to it," said the glue.
"Try to make a good impression," said the sealing wax.
And that's why the kettle sings as she works, and works as she sings.

HERBERT V. PROCHNOW

A teenager complained to a friend: "My dad wants me to have all the things he never had when he was a boy—including five straight A's on my report card."

"Young man," said the angry father from the head of the stairs, "didn't I hear the clock strike four when you brought my daughter in?"

"You did," admitted the boyfriend. "It was going to strike eleven, but I grabbed it and held the gong so it wouldn't disturb you."

The father muttered, "Wonder why I didn't think of that one in my courting days!"

GRIT

Making a great sacrifice nowadays means doing without things our parents never had.

THE BOY AND HIS WORLD

A boy had been given a beautiful globe of the world, and the little fellow became so interested in it the first evening that he insisted upon taking it into his room and placing it on a table beside his bed.

Later that evening the boy's parents got into a discussion of some far country, and the father said he would slip into the lad's room and bring out the globe so they could find the place in which they were interested.

Tiptoeing into the room, the father picked up the globe and was making his way toward the door when his son aroused and inquired sleepily: "Hey, Daddy, what are you doing with my world?"

SOURCE UNKNOWN

We are living in a day when young people are encouraged to believe that they are infinitely wiser than their elders. Of course growing boys and girls have always had a bit of this, but it is rather more so today. It should be remembered that young people have not yet been old, but older people have been young. So older people understand younger people better than younger people understand older people.

J.C. MACAULAY

Any other society at any other time would find teenagers like ours fully productive members of the community—earning a living and raising a family. Yet in an age when students are brighter than ever before, better educated, and more concerned about a contributing role in society, we continue to treat them as young children rather than young adults.

GREGORY R. ANRIG

TEENAGERS ARE TEMPORARY

A father was upset because his wife gave permission for their eighth grade daughter to have a date to a school party. Naturally, he went around making noises as an irate father is wont to do. When the boy showed up, a full six feet tall height, good old dad went into orbit. He fumed and groaned all evening, uttering dire warnings to his wife about what he'd do if anything happens."

Finally, on the dot at 9:30 PM—when the young Cinderella had been told to be home—there was a telephone call. "Daddy," the daughter blurted, "The positively worst thing has happened."

"What did he do?!" the father shouted.

"You'll have to come and get me," the daughter said. "His mother came and got him at nine o'clock.

ANONYMOUS

BILL OF RIGHTS

1. The right to the affection and intelligent guidance of understanding parents.
2. The right to be raised in a decent home in which he or she is adequately fed, clothed, and sheltered.
3. The right to the benefits of religious guidance and training.
4. The right to a school program, which, in addition to sound academic training, offers maximum opportunity for individual development and preparation for living.

5. The right to receive constructive discipline for the proper development of good character, conduct, and habits.
6. The right to be secure in his or her community against all influences detrimental to wholesome development.
7. The right to the individual selection of free and wholesome recreation.
8. The right to live in a community in which adults practice the belief that the welfare of their children is of primary importance.
9. The right to receive good adult example.

SOURCE UNKNOWN

Impressing upon his class an admiration for notable feats of physical prowess, the teacher related the exploit of a vigorous man who swam three times across a broad river, in the morning before breakfast.

There was a giggle from one of the youngsters in the class.

"Well," said the teacher with some irritation, "what is it that seems so amusing? I see nothing amusing."

"It's only this, sir, "replied the pupil, "I was wondering why he didn't make it four times and get back on the side where he left his clothes."

The following dialogue was overheard between a teenage son and parent:

"I'm off to the party."

"Well, have a good time."

"Look pop, don't tell me what to do."

THE RAILWAY CLERK

A teenager speaks:

At eleven years: "My parents are grand. They know everything."

At sixteen: "Really and truly, my parents are not quite so good as I used to think. They don't know everything."

At nineteen: "Although my parents think they are always right, they really know very little compared with what I know already."

At twenty-two: "My parents do not understand young people; they have nothing in common with the younger generation."

At thirty: "To tell the truth, my parents were right in many things."

At fifty: "My parents were wonderful people. They had a clear mind and always did the necessary things at the right moment, my beloved parents.

ANONYMOUS

I've taught our children that having money is no excuse for not doing a fair share of work. All the children had regular chores around the house, and they were expected to do them without question.

LAWRENCE WELK

I don't have to look up my family tree, because I know that I'm the sap.

FRED ALLEN

In my mind (Oliver Wiswell thought) there were thoughts of a thousand things I could have done for my father and hadn't. Ah—and the thoughts of the things I hadn't said to him! Never once had I told him how I admired him, loved him. My whole life seemed to have been spent in taking all from him and giving nothing! Why hadn't I once—just once—told him what I so deeply and truly knew him to be—the best and nicest man in the world! No such word had ever come from me.

KENNETH ROBERTS

TEENAGERS ARE TEMPORARY

Build me a son, O Lord, who will be strong enough to know when he is weak, and brave enough to face himself when he is afraid. One who will be proud and unbending in defeat but humble and gentle in victory.

A son whose wishbone will not be where his backbone should be; a son who will know that to know himself is the foundation stone of knowledge.

Rear him, I pray, not in the paths of ease and comfort but under the stress and spur of difficulties and challenges. Here let him learn compassion for those who fail.

Build me a son whose heart will be clean, whose goal will be high. A son who will master himself before he seeks to master other men. One who will learn to laugh, yet never forget how to weep. One who will reach into the future, yet never forget the past.

And after all these are his, add I pray, enough of a sense of humor so that he may always be serious, yet never take himself too seriously; a touch of humility, so that he may always remember the simplicity of true greatness; the open mind of true wisdom; the meekness of true strength.

Then, I, his father, will dare to whisper, "I have not lived in vain."

GENERAL DOUGLAS MACARTHUR

III

I will study and prepare myself, and someday my chance will come.
ABRAHAM LINCOLN

Father (looking over his son's report card): "One thing is in your favour. With these grades, you couldn't possibly be cheating!

TEENAGERS ARE TEMPORARY

The dean of a certain school wouldn't allow the star football player to play in the big game coming up Saturday. The coach brought the player into the dean's office and cried: "Why don't you let him play Saturday—We need him!"

"I tell you why," snapped the dean. "This is supposed to be a school of learning. All he knows is football, and I'll show you how ignorant he is!"

Then he said to the player: "Tell me, how much is two and two?"

"Seven." came the answer.

With that the coach cried to the dean: "Aw let him play. After all, he only missed it by one!"

ANONYMOUS

If anyone ever asks you whatever happened to the old-fashioned student who worked his way through college?" You can answer, "He's still here, and there is more of him than ever before."

DR. GEORGE BROWN

A student who continually watched the wall clock in English class got on the teacher's nerves.

Finally, the teacher mounted a sign over the clock: "Time will pass—will you?"

ANONYMOUS

A mother asked the dean of admissions if her son's excellence on the rock and roll guitar would carry any weight in getting him into college.

"Five years ago, maybe yes," he replied. "But now we are looking for some listeners."

C. KENNEDY

One of the greatest and most comforting of truths is that when one door closes another opens; but often we look so long and regretfully upon the closed door that we do not see the one that has opened for us.

Defeat is nothing but education; it is the first step toward something better.

ANONYMOUS

Rejected by the college of his choice, the teenager angrily accosted his father. "If you really cared for me, you'd have pulled some wires!"

"I know," replied the parent sadly. "The T.V., the hi-fi and the telephone would have done for a start."

DAISY BROWN

When I was a student,
I was quiet.
I didn't protest,
I didn't riot.

I wasn't unwashed,
I wasn't obscene,
I made no demands
on proxy or dean.

TEENAGERS ARE TEMPORARY

I sat in no sit-in,
I heckled no speaker,
I broke not a window . . .
Few students were meeker.

I'm forced to admit,
with some hesitation,
All I got out of school
was an education.

RICHARD ARMOUR

TEENAGERS ARE TEMPORARY

A bright student who lived near Cape Canaveral was asked by the teacher to count to ten by two's

"Yes ma'am—20—18—16—14—12—10."

LANE OLINGHOUSE

It is a wise student who has learned that passing a course in school is more important than passing a car on the highway.

Education is something you get when your father sends you to college, but it isn't complete until you send your own child.

Manhood and womanhood, not scholarship, is the first aim in education.

ERNEST THOMPSON SETON

No person really becomes a fool until he or she stops asking questions.

CHARLES STEINMETZ

Perhaps the most valuable result of all education is the ability to make yourself do the thing you have to do, when it ought to be done, whether you like it or not. It is the first lesson that ought to be learned.

THOMAS H. HUXLEY

The young man who worked so hard to graduate later wonders what the hurry was.

All who have meditated on the art of governing mankind have been convinced that the fate of empires depends on the education of youth.

ARISTOTLE

A teacher asked her class in ancient history, "What do you think Alexander the Great would be doing if he were alive today?"

"He'd be drawing old-age pension," the student said.

How are you getting along in school?"

"Oh, I'm as famous as Napoleon."

"How come?"

"I went down in history."

Question: How do you spell relief?

Answer: "G-R-A-D-U-A-T-I-O-N."

IV

Friends are a second existence.

Baltasar Gracian

Oh! be thou blest with what
Heaven can send,
Long health, long youth, long pleasure—and a friend.

ALEXANDER POPE

"My boy," a father advised his son, "treat everybody with politeness, even those who are rude to you. For remember that you show courtesy to others not because they are gentlemen, but because you are one."

TEENAGERS ARE TEMPORARY

Let dogs delight to bark and bite,
For God both made them so;
Let bears and lions growl and fight,
For 'tis their nature to. . . .

But you should never let
Such angry passions rise,
Your hands were never made
To tear each other's eyes.

ISAAC WATTS

"So in everything, do to others what you would have them do to you, for this sums up the Law and the Prophets."

MATTHEW 7:12

THE TEN COMMANDMENTS OF HUMAN RELATIONS

   I. Speak to people. There is nothing as nice as a cheerful word of greeting.
  II. Smile at people. It takes seventy-two muscles to frown, only fourteen to smile.
 III. Call people by name. The sweetest music to anyone's ears is the sound of his or her own name.
 IV. Be friendly and helpful.
  V. Be cordial. Speak and act as if everything you do is a genuine pleasure.

VI. Be genuinely interested in people. You can like almost everybody if you try.

VII. Be generous with praise—cautious with criticism.

VIII. Be considerate with the feelings of others. There are usually three sides to a controversy: yours, the other person's and the right one.

IX. Be alert to give service. What counts most in life is what we do for others.

X. Add to this a good sense of humor, a big dose of patience and a dash of humility, and you will be rewarded manyfold.

SOURCE UNKNOWN

The Chinese have a story based on three or four thousand years of civilization—

Two Chinese laborers were arguing heatedly in the midst of a crowd. A stranger expressed surprise that no blows were being struck.

His Chinese friend replied, "The man who strikes first admits that his ideas have given out."

FRANKLIN DELANO ROOSEVELT

V

If it were not for hope the heart would break.

ANONYMOUS

It would appear that our nature is not, for any length of time, capable of perfect resignation. Hope will make its way into the mind, and with hope, activity, and with activity, the realization of hope.

GOETHE

Hope is the better half of courage. Hope has it not sustained the work and given the fainting heart time and patience to outwit the chances and changes of life.

HONORE DE BALZAR

The greatest mistake you can make in this life is to be continually fearing you will make one.

ELBERT HUBBARD

Perhaps the most arresting bit of personal advice I ever encountered was this! If you want to be popular, live so that a blind person would like you.

The point is that lasting popularity depends not on having good looks or other surface personality traits, but your inner qualities that somehow communicate themselves to others.

Such qualities include a friendly voice, kindness, thoughtfulness of the other person's tender ego, sincere praise, gratitude, and encouragement.

HOW WELL WOULD A BLIND PERSON LIKE YOU?

The person who would control others must be able to control himself—He refuses to become rattled, to fly off in a temper, to stomp and holler and swear.

B.C. FORBES

TEENAGERS ARE TEMPORARY

Never say, "Oh well, I'm beaten!"
Never say, "I guess I'm done."
Say "I'll show 'em all tomorrow"
Say "The fight is just begun."

Never say, "My work has got me."
Never say, "I've lost my stride."
Say "I'm not much to look at,
But I've got the right stuff inside!"

Never let the world disarm you;
If folks put you on a shelf,
Just refuse to stay! Don't falter—
Have a little pride in yourself!!

CAROL SHERIDAN

I would be true,
For there are those who trust me;

I would be pure,
For there are those who care;

I would be strong,
For there is much to suffer;

I would be brave,
For there is much to dare;

TEENAGERS ARE TEMPORARY

I would be friend to all—
The foe, the friendless;

I would be giving,
And forget the gift;

I would be humble,
For I know my weakness;

I would look up—
And laugh—and love—and lift.

HOWARD A. WHEELER

The Roman philosopher and Statesman, Cicero, said this some 2,000 years ago, and it still holds true. The six mistakes of man:

1. The delusion that personal gain is made by crushing others.
2. The tendency to worry about things that cannot be changed or corrected.
3. Insisting that a thing is impossible because we cannot accomplish it.
4. Refusing to set aside trivial preferences.
5. Neglecting development and refinement of the mind, and not acquiring the habit of reading and study.
6. Attempting to compel others to believe and live as we do.

ANONYMOUS

A boy has a strong desire in his heart to be treated as a person of worth, to be respected for his maturity of judgment, for being a worthwhile, useful person. The process of growing up reaches throughout many years and that boy is fortunate indeed who counts among his friends a few understanding people who make clear to him that they respect him and believe in him, friends who encourage him to search for basic life values.

WALTER MACPEEK

People range from animals to gods.
They pray for you and prey on you.
They are bears for punishment and brutes for revenge.
Their restlessness fills them with wonderings and spurs them into
    wanderings.
They are creatures of moods and modes.
They try to look different, but deep down they all look alike.
They are hero-worshippers and idol-destroyers.
They are quick to take sides and quick to switch from side to side.
They like individuals who can appraise and praise them.
People must be taken as they are and still they want to be taken as
    they aren't.

They have their ways and want to get away with them.

They cry for the moon and wait for a place in the sun.

They are happiest in the hurly-burly giving and taking, making and
losing, to the tune of the hurdy-gurdy.

They try everything once and seldom stop to think twice.

But they are blessed with nine lives and often strike twelve at the
eleventh hours.

With people all things are possible, without them, all things are
impossible.

They must forever be felt and dealt with. To lose contact with them is
to lose contact with life.

Source Unknown

VI

Be not simply good; be good for something.

HENRY DAVID THOREAU

"What do you want to be when you grow up?" asked the visitor of his host's teenage son.

"I want to be possible," was the boy's quick reply.

"Possible?" said the visitor, perplexed.

"Yes," said the boy. "Every day somebody tells me I'm impossible!"

So nigh is the grandeur to our dust,
So near is God to man,
When Duty whispers low "Thou must,"
The youth replies, "I can."

RALPH WALDO EMERSON

Someone has advanced the theory that the best way to break a habit is to drop it.

"Beverage Alcohol," said the doctor who knew whereof he spoke, "gives you a red nose, a black eye, a white liver, a yellow streak, a green brain, a dark brown breath and a blue outlook."

A woodpecker was pecking away at the trunk of a dead tree. Suddenly, lightning struck the tree and splintered it.

The woodpecker flew away, unharmed. Looking back to where the dead tree had stood, the proud bird exclaimed, "Look what I did!"

VII

If A equals success, then the formula is A equals X plus Y and Z, with X being work, and Y play and Z keeping your mouth shut.

ALBERT EINSTEIN

TEENAGERS ARE TEMPORARY

We were born to succeed, not to fail.
HENRY DAVID THOREAU

O Lord,
Thou givest us everything,
at the price
of an effort.

LEONARDO DA VINCI

There is no right way to do a wrong thing.

The man who moved the mountain began by carrying away small stones.

ANONYMOUS

You don't lose your shirt by rolling up your sleeves.

TEENAGERS ARE TEMPORARY

If happiness truly consisted in physical ease and freedom from care,
then the happiest individual would not be either a man or a woman;
it would be, I think, an American cow.

WILLIAM LYON PHELPS

Wisdom is knowing what to do next; virtue is doing it.

DAVID STARR JORDON

Four things came not back:
The spoken word;
The sped arrow;
Time past;
The neglected opportunity.

Source Unknown

People do not lack strength; they lack will.

VICTOR HUGO

Folks who never do any more than they get paid for, never get paid for any more than they do.

ELBERT HUBBARD

Before God's footstool to confess
A poor soul knelt and bowed his head.
"I failed," he wailed. The master said.
"Thou didst thy best—that is success."

ANONYMOUS

TEENAGERS ARE TEMPORARY

Isn't it strange
That princes and kings
And clowns that caper
In sawdust rings,
And common people
Like you and me
are builders for eternity?

Each is given a bag of tools
A shapeless mass,
A book of rules;
And each must make,
Ere life is flown,
a stumbling-block
or a stepping-stone.

R.L. SHARPE

In building a firm foundation for success, here are the stones to remember.

> The wisdom of preparation.
> The value of confidence.
> The worth of honesty.
> The privilege of working.
> The discipline of struggle.
> The magnetism of character.
> The forcefulness of simplicity.
> The radiance of health.
> The winsomeness of courtesy.
> The attractiveness of modesty.

The inspiration of cleanliness.
The satisfaction of sewing.
The power of suggestion.
The buoyancy of enthusiasm.
The advantage of initiative.
The virtue of patience.
The rewards of cooperation.
The fruitfulness of perseverance.
The sportsmanship of losing.
The joy of winning.

Source Unknown

Handel lost his health. His right side was paralyzed. His money was gone. His creditors threatened to imprison him. Handel was so disheartened by his tragic experiences that he almost lost his faith and despaired. He came through the ordeal, however, and composed his greatest work "The Hallelujah Chorus," which is the climatic part of his great *Messiah.*

Keep your eye on the ball;
your shoulder to the wheel;
your ear to the ground.
Now, let's see you work in that position.

"When it is definitely settled that a thing can't be done, watch somebody do it."

This reminds us of what is said to have been the life motto of the late President Eliot of Harvard:
It can't be done;
It never has been done;
Therefore I will do it.

TEENAGERS ARE TEMPORARY

On a Friday morning an eager young person from Stanford University stood before Louis Janin, seeking part-time employment.

"All I need right now," said Janin, " is a stenographer."

"I'll take the job," said the eager applicant, "but I can't come back until next Tuesday."

On Tuesday, the young person reported for duty. "Why couldn't you come back before Tuesday?" Janin wanted to know.

"Because I had to rent a typewriter and learn how to use it!" was the unexpected answer.

That young person was Herbert Hoover who later became President of the United States.

WALTER B. KNIGHT

Most of us think we could move mountains if someone would clear the hills out of the way.

Said one little chick, with a funny little squirm, "I wish I could find a nice fat worm!"

Said a second little chick with a queer little shrug, "I wish I could find a nice fat bug."

Said a third little chick with a strange little squeal, "I wish I could find some nice yellow meal."

"Now look here," said the mother from the green garden patch, "If you want any breakfast, you must get up and scratch!"

TEENAGERS ARE TEMPORARY

I won't—is a tramp,
I can't—is a quitter
I don't know—is lazy,
I wish I could—is a wisher.

I might—is waking up,
I will try—is on his feet,
I can—is on the way,
I will—is at work,
I did—is the boss.

EARL CASSEL

VIII

Veni, Vidi, Vici—I came, I saw, I conquered.

JULIUS CAESAR

TEENAGERS ARE TEMPORARY

To get ahead
You first should stare
Until you're sure
The stairs are there.
And then with vigor
And finesse
Climb up
The stairway
To success

THOMAS CARLYLE

Success is not a matter of luck. It is mainly a matter of first, work; second, work; third, work—with, of course, a plentiful mixture of brain, foresight, and imagination. Remember also, that genius is most times the fruit of hard work—well directed and long-visioned.

B.C. FORBES

What a boy cares about is often more important than what he knows. How he feels, down inside, about himself, and how he feels toward other people can be of far more importance than his actual performance at the moment. Attitudes are important because they become the basis of lifelong conduct.

WALTER MACPEEK

Our greatest glory is not in never falling but in rising everytime we fall.

CONFUCIUS

The snow covered the ground, and three lads were playing. A man came and said to them: "Would you like to try a race, and the winner gets a prize?"

The boys agreed, and the man told them that his race would be different. "I will go to the other side of the field," he said, "and when I give you the signal, you will start to run. The one whose footsteps are straightest in the snow will be the winner."

The race began, and the first boy kept looking at his feet to see if his steps were straight. The second lad kept looking at his companions to see what they were doing. But the third boy ran on with his eyes steadfastly fixed on the man on the other side of the field.

The third lad was the winner, for his footsteps were straight in the snow. He had kept his eyes firmly on the goal.

GRIT

Mickey Mantle, on his baseball career:

"During my 18 years as a baseball player, I came to bat almost 10,000 times. I struck out 1,700 times and walked maybe 1,800 times. You figure a ball player will average about 500 hits a season. That means I played seven years in the major league without even hitting a ball."

SPORTS ILLUSTRATED

A six year old lad came home with a note from his teacher suggesting that he be taken out of school, as he was "too stupid to learn." The boy's name was Thomas A. Edison.

Alfred Tennyson's grandfather gave him ten shillings for writing an elegy on his grandmother. Handing it to the boy, the old man said: "There, that's the first money you ever earned by your poetry, and take my word for it, it will be the last."

Benjamin Franklin's mother-in-law hesitated about letting her daughter marry a printer. There were already two printing offices in the United States, and she feared the country might not be able to support a third.

SOURCE UNKNOWN

There's joy in the world,
If you but find it;
There's a Voice to guide,
If we but mind it.
There's a pot of gold at the rainbow's end—
Waits the heart's desire round
The road's last bend.

MARY E. F. POCK

Someone has compiled the following 10 excuses that are not recommended for ambitious men and women:

1. That is the way we've always done it.
2. I didn't know you were in a hurry for it.
3. That's not in my department.
4. No one told me to go ahead.
5. I'm waiting for an O.K.
6. How did I know this was different.
7. That's his job, not mine.
8. Wait till the boss comes back and ask him.
9. I forgot.
10. I didn't think it was important.

GRIT

Every boy deep down in his heart would like to be a hero—to himself, to his fellows, to people around him. He sometimes likes to picture himself in the limelight—being seen and heard and looked up to—respected and admired. He visualizes himself frequently as a saver of life, as a protector and defender of the weak, as a young man of courage and strength. But most of all, he pictures himself as being a respected, useful, worthwhile man.

WALTER MACPEEK

First Scout: "Has your troop ever gotten lost in the woods?"

Second Scout: "No, but we were confused for three days once!"

To be what we are, and to become what we are capable of becoming, is the only end in life.

BENEDICT DE SPINOZA

God gives every bird its food, but He does not throw it in the nest.

SOURCE UNKNOWN

For when the One Great Scorer comes
To write against your name,
He writes—not that you won or lost—
But how you played the game.

GRANTLAND RICE

The poor person is not the one without a cent but the one who is without a dream.

HARRY KEMP

The Duke of Wellington is reported to have said, "The British are not braver than the French—they are only brave for five minute's longer."

We are not driven from Behind,
But lured from Before!
Not pushed, not pulled!
Magnetized from beyond!

LLOYD C. DOUGLAS

Do more than exist—live.
Do more than touch—feel.
Do more than look—observe.
Do more than read—absorb.
Do more than hear—listen.
Do more than listen—understand.
Do more than think—ponder.
Do more than talk—say something.

SOURCE UNKNOWN

TEENAGERS ARE TEMPORARY

My grandfather in his house of logs
Said the young folks are going to the dogs,
His grandfather in the Flemish bogs
Said the young folks are going to the dogs.

And his grandfather in his long skin togs
Said the young folks are going to the dogs!
There is but one thing I have to state:
The dogs are having a mighty long wait!

ANONYMOUS

There is a tide in the affairs of men
Which, taken at flood, leads on
to fortune;
Omited, all the voyage of their life
Is bound in shallows and in miseries.

WILLIAM SHAKESPEARE

There are six things that "Keeps us Going":

First, the instinct to live, which we apparently have no part in making or deciding about.

Second, group consciousness and the desire that we have to win the approbation of our fellows within the group.

Third, the various interests that we may find in life, such as religion or art or some such other branch of aesthetics.

Fourth, in our climate, the habit of work.
Fifth, the sheer joy we find in hours of well-earned recreation after
    hard work—games, fishing, tramping the hills, a good book.
Sixth, and most important, the general feeling that we have that
    there is some abstract goodness or rightness in the world with
    which we cooperate in making the world a fine place for a
    splendid race of men, women and children to live in.

SOURCE UNKNOWN

TEENAGERS ARE TEMPORARY

Three men were laying brick.

The first was asked: ' What are you doing?"
He answered "Laying some brick."

The second was asked: "What are you working for?"
He answered: "Five dollars a day."

The third man was asked: "What are you doing?"
He answered: "I am building a great cathedral."

CHARLES M. SCHWAB

American youth can be trusted.

JOSEPH F. KENNEDY

IX

Love is friendship set on fire.-

JEREMY TAYLOR

TEENAGERS ARE TEMPORARY

You can carry a pack
If it's strapped on your back;
You can carry a weight in your hands,
You can carry a bundle
On the top of you head,
As they in other lands.

A load is light
If you carry it right,
Though it weighs as much as a boulder;
But a tiny chip
Is too heavy to bear
If you carry it on your shoulder.

Source Unknown

Father chanced to enter the room just as fourteen year old Junior broke open his 'piggy bank.'

"Hey there!" said Dad, "You should think of the future, son, and save your money."

"I know, Dad," replied Junior, counting out the change, "but it's my girlfriend's birthday, and I've got to think of the present."

F. G. KERMAN

A very bashful young man called on his girlfriend, bringing with him a large bouquet of flowers and a big box of chocolates. When he presented her with the gifts, she threw her arms around him and kissed him resoundingly. Immediately, he turned to leave the room.

"I'm so sorry," she said contritely, "If I did something wrong."

"Oh," he replied, "You didn't do anything wrong. I'm just going out for some more flowers and candy."

JOAN I. WELSH

TEENAGERS ARE TEMPORARY

Slipping ice, very thin.
Pretty girl tumbled in.
Saw a boy upon the bank—
Gave a shriek, and then she sank.

Boy on bank heard her shout,
jumped right in—helped her out.
Now they're lovers—very nice,
But first she had to break the ice.

HERBERT V. PROCHNOW

Teenage boys who whistle at girls are just going through a stage which will probably last fifty years.

Required of every good lover—The Whole Alphabet:

Agreeable—Bountiful—Constant—Dutiful—Easy—Faithful—Gallant
—Honorable—Ingenious—Joyful—Kind—Loyal—Mild—Noble—
Officious—Prudent—Quiet —Rich—Secret—True—Understanding—
Valiant—Wise—X (anything you want to include)—Young—
Zealous.

MIGUEL DE CERVANTES

There is no grief which time does not lessen and soften.

CICERO

'Tis better to have loved and lost
Than never to have loved at all.

TENNYSON

HER — "I will not until I find a man with the courage of a lion but the meekness of a lamb; the wisdom of Socrates but the cleverness of Noel Coward; he must be as handsome as a movie star but never conceited; he must be as gallant as Sir Walter Raleigh, but . . . ."

HIM — "How fortunate we met."

A young man went into a jewelry store to look at an engagement ring. Pointing to a sparkling diamond, he asked the price.

"That one there is $1,000.00," replied the jeweler.

The young man looked startled and let out a whistle.

Pointing to another ring, he said, "And this one?"

The jeweler replied "That one is two whistles."

X

To satisfy the itch for money — scratch for it!

The darkest hour in the history of any young person is when he or she sits down to study how to get money without earning it.—
HORACE GREELY

A young man called one evening on a rich old farmer to learn the farmer's story of how he became rich. "It's a long story," said the old man, "and while I'm telling it, we might as well save the candle," and he blew the candle out.

"You needn't go on," said the young man, "I understand!"
SOURCE UNKNOWN

"I don't like money, actually, but it quiets my nerves."

JOE LOUIS

TEENAGERS ARE TEMPORARY

The wealth of the world
Isn't found in its streams;
It lies on its people
and all of their dreams.

Imagine the world with its gold,
If you can,
But without the high-thinking
Courage of man!

You can sum its resources
again and again,
But the wealth of the world
Is its women and men.

ANONYMOUS

The farmer was telling about a herder who was developing a strain of sheep for speed. "He tells me that he's got a lamb now that can run 85 miles an hour."

"But why does he want lambs that can go 85 miles an hour?" inquired the young daughter.

"So they can keep up with Mary."

Uncle: "And what are you going to be when you grow up, Freddy?"

Freddy: "I'm going to be a philanthropist, they always have lots of money!"

XI

A horse! A horse! My kingdom for a horse!

WILLIAM SHAKESPEARE

A reckless driver drives as though he owned the road while the careful driver acts like he owned his car.

If you sleep in a chair,
You have nothing to lose;
But a nap at the wheel
Is a permanent snooze

HERBERT V. PROCHNOW

A father who visited his son at college asked him what he wanted for his birthday. The son replied that he wanted a new car. His father, looking at the college parking lot, said, "Look at all these ancient jalopies. Your present car is in much better shape than any of them."

The college student replied, "Those old cars don't belong to the students. They belong to the professors."

Daddy, What is a bachelor?

A bachelor, my boy, is a man who didn't have a car when he was young.

SOURCE UNKNOWN

A young man was arrested while necking with his girlfriend on a freeway. He was charged with driving while "infatuated."

TEENAGERS ARE TEMPORARY

GIVE ME A HORSE

O horse you are a wonderful thing;
No buttons to push, no horn to honk;
You start yourself, no clutch to slip;
No spark to miss, no gears to strip;
No license buying every year
With plates to screw on front and rear;
No gas bills climbing up each day,
Stealing the joy of life away;
No speed cops chugging in your rear
Yelling summons in your ear.

TEENAGERS ARE TEMPORARY

Your inner tubes are all okay.
And thank the Lord, they stay that way;
Your spark plugs never miss and fuss
Your motor never makes us cuss.
Your frame is good for many a mile;
Your body never changes style.
Your wants are few and easy met
You've something on the auto yet.

GIVE ME A HORSE!

Source Unknown

Ten little autos, road and weather fine; one hit a culvert—then there
were nine.

Nine little autos, one a little late; driver struck a railroad train—then
there were eight.

Seven little autos speeding through the sticks; one skidded off the
road—then there were six.

Six little autos till one took a dive through a open drawbridge—then
there were five.

Five little autos, one with rattling door; driver tried to shut it—then
there were four.

Four little autos, one climbed a tree; but didn't do it very well—so
    that left only three.
Three little autos, one driver was a "stew"; loaded up on highball—
    that left only two.
Two little autos, tried to beat the gun when the warning signal
    flashed—then there was one.
One little auto around the corner tore; hit a truck—that's all there is;
    there isn't any more!

Source Unknown

XII

Remember your Creator in the days of your youth.
ECCLESIASTES 12:1

More things are wrought by prayer than the world dreams of.
Wherefore, let thy voice
Rise like a fountain for me night and day.
For what are men better than sheep or goats
That nourish a blind life within the brain.
If knowing God, they lift not hands of prayer
Both for themselves and those who they call friend?

ALFRED, LORD TENNYSON

I believe in teenagers. I believe in teenagers because they make mistakes, just as their fathers did.

I believe in teenagers because they are our future. They start out clean, eagerly. They want to win. They do not want to lose.

I believe in teenagers because they are growing. They outgrow their clothes, but they also outgrow their childish ideas, habits, and childishness. They are dynamic.

I believe in teenagers because they are a good investment. I cannot give them much money, but I can give them a lot of love, understanding, and concern.

A teenager wakes up when he meets Jesus Christ. Up to that time, his life has been a protected, cloistered one in which the necessities have been provided through no effort of his own. His clothing, food, housing all have been given to him by conscientious providers known as parents. Now that he has come into the age of decision and maturity of mentality, his horizons can be unlimited.

J. LESTER HARNISH

Christ appeals to young people because of their need for love. Everyone needs love, but the need is accentuated in the experience of youth. They cover this need up rather effectively because they are afraid they won't be loved. But the need is there.

Christ appeals to young people because of their need for forgiveness. I do not know any group of individuals who get more uptight about their imperfections.

Christ appeals to young people's need for the meaning of life. The thing that makes Christ appealing to young people is that he can bring meaning and joy and hope, even in a world like ours. They are attracted by a God who came into this imperfect world and lived in it and brought meaning and hope where there is imperfection and sin.

KENNETH CHAFIN

The Lord bless you and
keep you;
The Lord make His face shine upon you
and be gracious unto you;
The Lord turn His face toward you
and give you peace.

NUMBERS 6:24-26